Mel Bay Presents

JAZZ VIOLA WIZARD JUNIOR

by Martin Norgaard

Edited by Laura Reed
Foreword by Darol Anger

Online Audio

To Access the Online Audo Go To:
www.melbay.com/20188BCDEB

1 2 3 4 5 6 7 8 9 0

Visit us on the Web at www.melbay.com — E-mail us at email@melbay.com

FOREWORD

Book, meet this string student/teacher. String student/teacher, meet this book. And welcome to one of the most exciting developments in string education since the tape recorder.

Since long before the National Standards in music education were introduced, there has been a great need for an elementary-level method for strings focusing on improvisation and America's great art music, jazz. *Jazz Fiddle Wizard Junior, Jazz Viola Wizard Junior,* and *Jazz Cello Wizard Junior* succeed in filling this gap, informing the string teacher while bringing students along, using familiar basic musical rules and principles.

String players need to feel like musicians within many styles of music, without leaving the classical style behind. This is not a difficult task, especially if addressed early, with the help of this book and other new resources.

Encouraging individual creativity and competence in various musical spheres will ensure a higher rate of string players staying with the instrument. As players mature, their wider abilities will allow them to follow their own musical preferences and continue playing, whether as professionals, semi-pros, or for personal enjoyment. Consequently, there will be more general interest in strings, and that seems like a good thing from here.

Martin Norgaard is in the vanguard of an upsurge and renewal of interest in strings, in a country that has made a habit of upsurge and renewal. This book and its advanced companion volume, *Jazz Fiddle Wizard,* are two key pieces in a new comprehensive curriculum that will bring string players into the larger musical world of the 21st century.

I know that both students and teachers will enjoy working with this method, and best of all, music will be made!

Darol Anger
January 2002

ABOUT THE ORIGINAL JAZZ FIDDLE WIZARD

"I have never seen a more clear, succinct method for string players. I'm not sure anything else could really be considered competition. If you have a stack of other jazz method books, lay them aside and buy this one. If you are considering whether you want to learn jazz, reading through this volume will give you an idea of the path you will have to take to be successful."

Hollis Taylor, violinist and writer for Strings *and* Fiddler *magazines*

"A musical adventure right from the very first page, this method is a winner."

Dr. John Kuzmich, Jr., Jazz Education Journal, *March 2001*

"Here is a good introduction to jazz improvisation for violinists."

George Brock, American String Teacher, *August 2001*

TABLE OF CONTENTS
ONLINE AUDIO TRACK NUMBERS

INTRODUCTION - TEACHER

Jazz Viola Wizard Junior is designed to teach by imitation. The Suzuki philosophy speaks about music as a language that can be learned in the same way we learn to speak. Throughout history, jazz was passed on to the next generation as an aural art form in jam sessions and by imitating recordings. *JVWjr* teaches students in the same way by emphasizing ear training and omitting a lot of explanation and analysis. *JVWjr* tells students to do something but leaves out why they are doing it. The original *Jazz Fiddle Wizard* (Mel Bay, 2000) includes analysis. If you have both books, compare each Lesson 1: *JVWjr* just has students imitate the rhythm they hear on the CD, while *JFW* shows an analysis of the triplet swing subdivision. *JVWjr* is designed for younger students who have played for about one year, while *JFW* was written for first-year college students who already have a classical or fiddle foundation.

You will find that very little is said about articulation in both books. The reason is that there is no right and wrong. Stephane Grappelli played smoothly with very few accents, while Stuff Smith used heavy accents, phrasing much like a horn. While listening to the CD, please notice that I phrase Lessons 1 and 2 and the blues piece with heavy bow pressure, little vibrato, and strong accents inspired by Smith. Lesson 3 and "Sweet Rose" are played with a lighter touch and more of a classical tone. This book, however, is about improvising, not the study of styles. That said, a strong effort should be made to focus students' attention on precise rhythm. In fact, this entire book is mostly about rhythm combined with pentatonic and major scales. The last lesson introduces the concept of the relationship between the improvised line and the chord in the accompaniment, a subject that will be explored further in subsequent titles.

In a private teaching studio, have the students read the lesson out loud including the explanation for the first track exercise. Make sure to quiz the students on what they just read. I find that many teenagers are good readers but sometimes don't comprehend what they just read. Ask questions such as "do you agree with that?" or "what does that mean?" Don't discourage students if they play more than what is actually asked for in a particular exercise—for example, if they improvise with skips to Track # 30, even though the book doesn't use skips until Track # 33. Point out to them that they are actually skipping ahead. Then do the original exercise again, challenging students by asking them to limit themselves to using exactly what is asked for. Limiting choices teaches control; control can later be used to expand choices.

Though you should have the book on a music stand in front of students, encourage them to turn away from the book and use their ears as much as possible. Tracks # 2 and # 9 may initially be skipped in favor of the subsequent exercises designed for use by ear only. These tracks were designed to teach students how certain jazz rhythms look on paper and foreshadow rhythms used in the following pieces.

As I gather feedback about this book including uses, ages, settings, etc., I will post these on my website www.JazzFiddleWizard.com. Please let me know how the book worked in your setting by sending me feedback and suggestions.

Martin Norgaard, January 2002
Martin@JazzFiddleWizard.com

INTRODUCTION - STUDENT

Go ahead, pop in the CD and listen. There are tracks you play along with and tracks that you answer. Sometimes you copy the question phrase, and sometimes you improvise the answer.

Now open the book to Lesson 1. You'll see that the exercises are listed as track numbers on the CD. On the exercises where it indicates Teacher and Student sections, you listen while I play the Teacher part and you play when it says Student. The book quickly gets harder and harder. Don't be afraid to repeat exercises many times if necessary. If you are more advanced, skip over some of the easy exercises. Make sure you always challenge yourself so you are not bored.

When you get to one of the pieces, first play along with the CD track that has me and my friend Paul playing the parts. Then try to play the different lines to the next track that only has the rhythm section. If you have friends who play a stringed instrument, you can all play together in any combination of violins, violas, and cellos as long as you all have the book for your instrument. Each line A, B, and C is identical in each book except the lines are written in the octave and clef that fits each instrument. First try with violins playing line A, violas line B, and cellos line C. Then try and swap so the cellos or the violas get the melody in line A. If you are part of a group of like instruments (all violins, all violas, or all cellos), simply decide who wants to play each line. There is also a piano part if one of your friends play keys. When you get to the improvised solo section, don't be scared. That's what you just practiced in the lesson. Have fun, and shoot me an email to let me know how it goes!

Martin Norgaard, January 2002
Martin@JazzFiddleWizard.com

WEBSITE

Visit www.JazzFiddleWizard.com for information on the history of jazz strings, a comprehensive discography, lesson plans, assessment tools, and course syllabi. Hear rare recordings of jazz violinists on the JazzFiddleWizard.com radio station.

ACKNOWLEDGMENTS

I would like to thank all the students and teachers that helped test this method: Sara Johnson, Dee Dee Besser, Ann Rudolph, and Paul Nelson. A special thanks to Renata Bratt for testing and help with the cello edition, to Darol Anger for a great foreword, to Paul Nelson for superb cello playing, and to Jim White for the drum grooves. Also thanks to my teenage students Cat and Chris Acree for letting me be a "fly on the wall" while they tested the book in a home study situation. My sincerest gratitude to Laura Reed, without whom I could not have written this book. She not only did a great job editing the text and music but also was instrumental in helping me adapt my ideas to middle school level.

SUPPLEMENTING A GROUP CURRICULUM WITH JVWJR

Jazz Viola Wizard Junior lends itself particularly well to group use, whether in a homogeneous Suzuki group lesson or a heterogeneous public school orchestra class. As a classically trained "reader" with no skills in improvisation, I was thrilled to find a supplemental method book that could help me approach the teaching of jazz to beginners.

When I first tried this book with my string students at John F. Kennedy Middle School in the Nashville suburb of Antioch, Tennessee, I found that the lessons worked best if I simply turned on the CD and let it run without stopping, giving only brief instructions in the few seconds between each track. In exercises requiring students to echo a question, all students played together. In exercises requiring an improvised answer to a question, I went around the room and assessed each student individually. For larger classes, I simply played the track twice to give each player a chance to shine.

My first- and second-year students performed the lessons better when they did not have the music in front of them. Even my fifth-grade beginners were able to play the rhythms in Lesson 1 without realizing that they were complicated. They instinctively imitated the strong, sticky tone that is modeled on the CD.

Most leading method books—such as *Suzuki School*, *Essential Elements*, and *Strictly Strings*—introduce F-natural and C-natural on the D and A strings in the last third of Book 1, but I introduce this new finger pattern much sooner in my teaching. Lesson 2 of *JVWjr* provides me with a motivating vehicle for reinforcing this skill. After spending some time teaching the D minor pentatonic scale by rote, my fifth graders are able to imitate and respond to the musical questions presented by the CD. While some of my sixth-grade (second-year) students were able to imitate the one- and two-bar questions on the first try, others required several repetitions. Even students who caught on quickly did not mind reviewing the exercises repeatedly, because they really enjoy the groove of the music!

The most common difficulty beginning students had with Lessons 2 and 3 was producing a healthy tone and keeping a steady beat while also thinking about adding notes with their left hands. If students simply could not imitate or answer the CD, I spent more time playing my own two- and three-note questions on one string for students to answer before moving on to motives involving more notes, two strings, or large skips. The empty backup tracks are ideal for creating additional exercises.

Older students (seventh and eighth grade) whom I inherited from another teacher had more difficulty than the younger students imitating the jazz style of the recording and were more shy about improvising in front of their peers. This observation only deepened my conviction to start students off learning the jazz dialect and improvising from the very beginning of their studies. Like learning any language, however, it's never too late to try.

For a long time I wondered how to introduce chord changes to middle school students without getting into too much theory; Lesson 4 of *JVWjr* provided my solution. When students ask questions about the Em and C7 chords, I try to be as brief as possible with my answers, explaining that we will get into the theory of it all later down the road. For now, I tell them, we need to simply concentrate on hearing when the B sounds better than the B-flat and visa versa. I am looking forward to subsequent *JVWjr* books that will provide further means of teaching students to play over chord changes without requiring college-level theory to understand it.

For my students who are strong readers, I encourage them to play as much of each lesson as possible without looking at their books. Conversely, students who play mostly by ear are encouraged to look at their music in order to learn to recognize some of the jazz rhythms that they will encounter in later pieces.

Jazz is a 20th-century art form often referred to as America's classical music—a fact that helps my students find the relevance of string playing to their lives. I look forward to learning to improvise in the jazz style along side of my students in the coming years.

Laura Reed
January 2002

LESSON 1:
IMPROVISING WITH RHYTHMS

Improvising is like talking. Players talk to each other using melody and rhythm. In a traditional jazz combo the soloist will trade rhythms back and forth with the piano player and the drummer. Just like people who talk without stopping, soloists who play without rests and cool rhythms will loose the interest of the audience. The eighth notes are swung. Listen to the CD to get the right feel. (Teacher: This entire lesson is built on eighth-note subdivision only. Often notes are accented. Use a martelé stroke to produce a characteristic jazz accent similar to a tongued note on saxophone. This page shows the relationship between jazz rhythm and articulation. The advanced student is encouraged to transfer these articulation principles to similar rhythms later in the book.)

Track # 1: Tuning note A

Track # 2: First let's just play some cool rhythms that are only a measure long. Watch the music and play along with the CD example, which repeats each rhythm four times.
(Teacher: use the piano accompaniment below but change the right hand rhythm for each example. You can also use the bass line and chord voicings from the solo section of "Wizard Blues," changing the rhythms to fit the following exercises.)

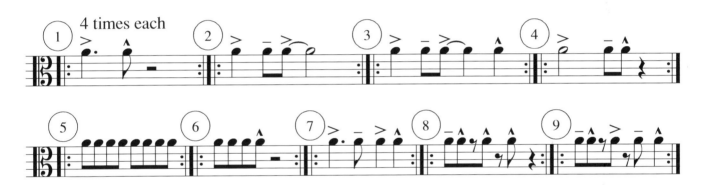

If you work with a pianist, the accompaniment to the first rhythm above would look like this:

Track # 3: TURN AWAY FROM THE BOOK AND USE YOUR EAR. Let's play "question and answer." First repeat the question by simply playing back the rhythm from the CD or your teacher.

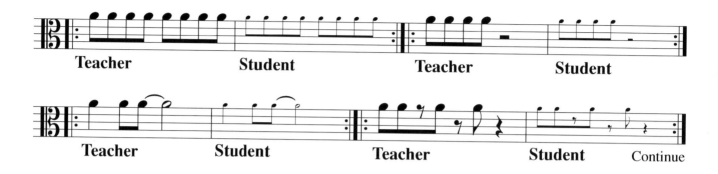

Track # 4: STILL WITHOUT LOOKING AT THE BOOK. This time answer by playing something different, as if you are answering the teacher or CD. Start making up rhythms that are not written. If you are part of a group, you can go around the room, each taking turns playing a different rhythm.

Sample

Track # 5: We now expand to two-measure question-and-answer rhythms. First, just repeat the question. DON'T LOOK, JUST USE YOUR EAR:

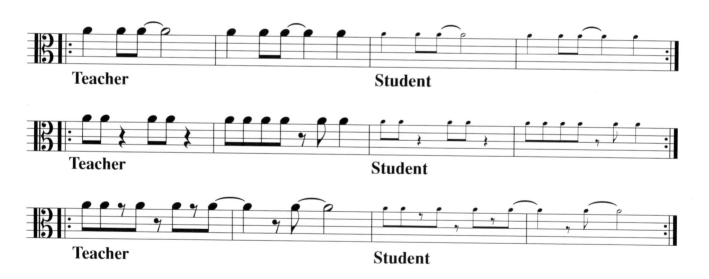

Track # 6: Now, answer the two-measure questions with a different rhythm:

Sample

Teacher   **Student**

Teacher   **Student**   Continue

Track # 7: You should now be ready to improvise a cool rhythm solo. Don't "talk" all the time. Try making up questions, then answer them yourself. You can also try to imitate talking by thinking of a sentence when you play. Below is an example. After playing along with the sample, keep going and make up your own solo. Use Track # 17 (backup only) if you are in a group:

Sample

Continue

In the next lesson we will add some melodies from the pentatonic scale. Then we'll play and improvise on "Wizard Blues." You'll find the rhythms in "Wizard Blues" very familiar!

LESSON 2:
IMPROVISING WITH RHYTHM
AND PITCH

Think of all the possibilities we discovered in Lesson 1 when we improvised using only rhythm. Now imagine the possibilities when we also change the pitch. First we'll practice the scale we will use for improvising. The scale is similar to choosing a subject to talk about. By limiting the improvising to only the notes in the D minor pentatonic scale (written below), we know any note will fit.

Track # 8: Let's play up and down the D minor pentatonic scale so we agree on our musical topic. Notice you always skip first finger and that both second fingers are low.

Track # 9: Now let's learn some small musical sentences combining the D minor pentatonic scale with our rhythms from Lesson 1. Watch the music and play along with the CD example, which repeats each measure four times.

(Teacher: For piano accompaniment, use the part below or the piano part from the solo section of "Wizard Blues.")

Track # 10: Now let's try by ear. Turn away from the book and see if you can imitate the question phrase. Hint: All these phrases start on the open D string and go straight up the scale:

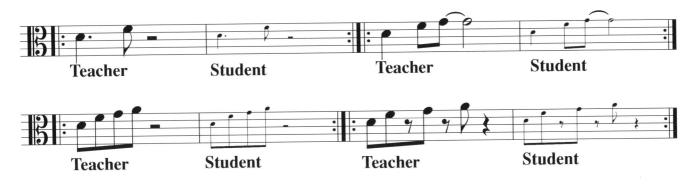

Track # 11: Here are a couple that start on the A string and go either up or down:

Track # 12: Can you pick these out? They start on D, but skip notes and change direction:

Track # 13: This time, the examples start on any note of the scale:

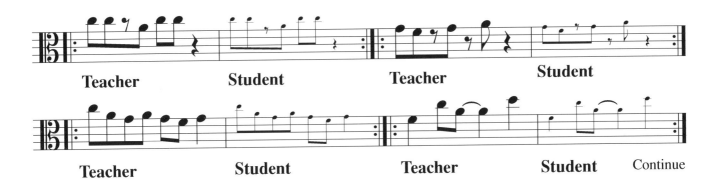

Track # 14: Now answer the melodic question differently BUT start on the same note the question phrase started on. Remember to play by ear and don't look at the book. The student part below is only a sample; you should make up something new each time you answer the CD or your teacher. (Teacher: If you are working with a group, you can assign pairs of students to play back and forth using the same start note.)

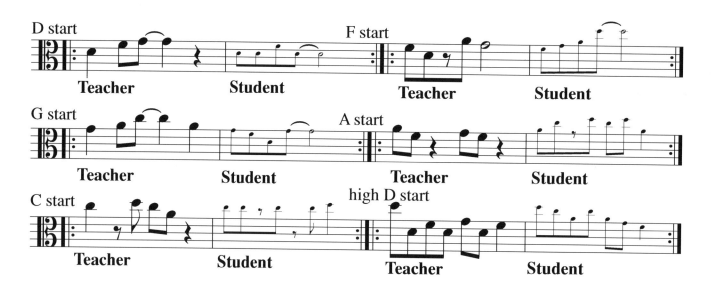

Track # 15: Now let's try with a two-measure question and answer. Choose your own starting note:

Track # 16: You should now be ready to improvise a short solo. Here we will play the Blues; traditional Blues melodies and lyrics are 12 measures long and are built on the question-and-answer principle. Remember that, just like with the rhythms in Lesson 1, you should always play with questions and answers within your solo. Here is an example:

CD continues with a regular
Blues solo

Track # 17: Go for it! This track has no solo instrument and goes through the Blues 12 times.

LESSON 2 (ADVANCED): ADDING THE BLUES NOTE AND EFFECTS

The following is for more advanced students. The solo in "Wizard Blues" can easily be played without the material below.

Track # 18: Flatting the fifth note of the minor pentatonic scale creates a scale called the Blues scale. The flat 5 is often referred to as the Blues note. Let's play the scale with the Blues note added:

Track # 19: Repeat after the CD or your teacher, by ear if you can, using the Blues note:

Teacher   **Student**   **Teacher**   **Student** Continue

Track # 20: Answer the CD or your teacher with a different phrase:

Teacher   **Student**   **Teacher**   **Student** Continue

Track # 21: Below are some advanced Bluesy effects you can use to spice up your solo. After playing each effect four times the CD plays a solo chorus using the effects.

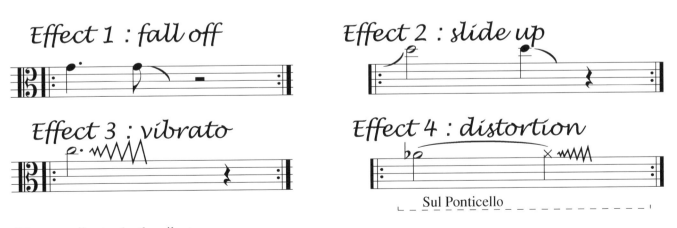

(Use arm vibrato. As the vibrato gets wider the finger leaves the string creating a harmonic effect.)

(Move the bow closer to the bridge and lift the finger off the string.)

Line A

WIZARD BLUES

M. Norgaard

Last time D.S. al Coda without repeats

WIZARD BLUES

Line B

M. Norgaard

Shuffle Blues ♩ = 120

Solos

(play background as needed)

(CD repeats solo 4 times)

Last time D.S. al Coda without repeats

WIZARD BLUES

M. Norgaard

Last time D.S. al Coda without repeats

WIZARD BLUES

Solos

Last time D.S. al Coda without repeats

LESSON 3:
USING THE ENTIRE SCALE

In this lesson you will improvise using the entire G major scale. Scales include all the notes we use when we play in a certain key. Practicing scales gives you a good foundation for improvising because it teaches the fingers how to stay within the key.

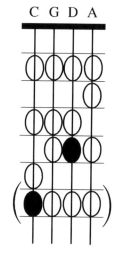

The G major scale, as you can see from the drawing, has high third finger on the C string, high second fingers on the G and D strings and low second finger on A.

Track # 24: Play the scale, first in quarters, then in swing eighths, then with a simple rhythm. (Use the lower line if you are playing by yourself with Track # 36, which is rhythm section only.)

piano repeats back to beginning

swing eighths

mixed rhythm

Track # 25: Apply the rhythms from Lesson 1 to our scale. Only part of the following exercises are written out. (Teacher: use Track # 36 [backup only] to play scales in full register or using other rhythms from Lesson 1.)

Continue

Track # 26: How about switching between two different rhythms:

Continue

Track # 27: You may now be able to play the scale in all eighth notes. Experiment with slurs as shown in the last measure. (Teacher: By phrasing with slurs, string players can swing without using heavy triplet-ization.)

Continue

Track # 28: Can you mix up many rhythms while you play the scale? After hearing or playing along with the sample, make up your own scale rhythms. Use Track # 36 to try this many times or with a group:

Continue

Track # 29: Now let's add another element of melodic improvisation. Instead of going straight up the scale, we will now change direction and descend before getting to the top of the scale, then ascend before getting to the bottom. In this and the following exercises, play along with the violin on the CD track then continue playing using the same principle after the violin stops:

Continue

Track # 30: Let's add rhythms. After playing along with the CD, continue to play adding your own rhythms to the scale.

Continue

Track # 31: How about starting on a note other than the low G:

Continue

Track # 32: Let's add repeated notes:

Continue

Track # 33: Now add skips within your scale. Make sure you stay within the scale using high third finger on the C string, and low second finger on the A string:

Continue

Track # 34: Using our new scale, play short two-measure questions and answers like we did in the previous lessons. Don't repeat the question, but play an answer that is RELATED to the question. Try to use what you've learned earlier in the lesson: cool rhythms, scale improvising starting on different notes, and adding skips. Only the first three questions are written out:

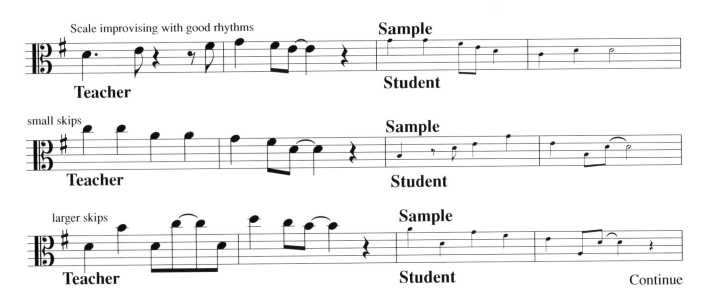

Game (not on CD): You can make a game out of this exercise by trying to start on the same note as the previous person ended on. Use Track # 36 (backup only):

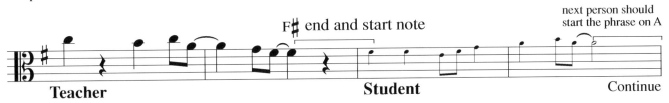

Track # 35: You should now be in good shape to improvise over the solo section of "Sweet Rose." Remember to "talk" to yourself in the solo by asking and answering your own questions. Here is a sample solo:

CD continues with a regular swing solo

Track # 36: Go for it! This track has no solo instrument and goes through the swing progression nine times.

LESSON 3 (ADVANCED): ADDING TRIPLETS AND SIXTEENTHS

The following is for more advanced students. The solo in "Sweet Rose" can easily be played without the material below.

Track # 37: Try adding triplet and sixteenth notes to your scale. First play a couple of scale drills similar to the beginning of the lesson except including faster notes. This track uses triplets. Do similar drills with sixteenths using Track # 36 (backup only). You can also use Track # 36 to try this exercise using the full register of your instrument in first position--that is, from low C up to D on the A string:

Track # 38: Try trading licks (questions and answers, as in Track # 34) that include triplets and sixteenths:

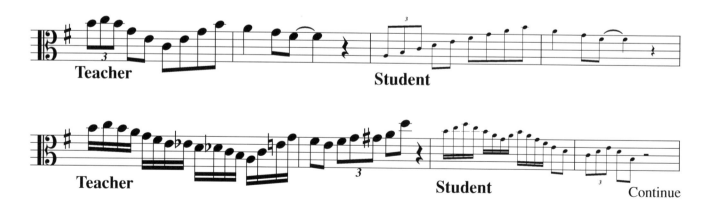

SWEET ROSE

Line A

SWEET ROSE

SWEET ROSE

SWEET ROSE

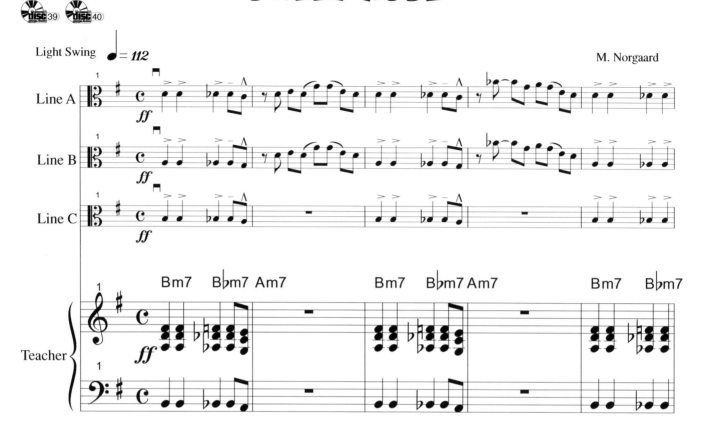

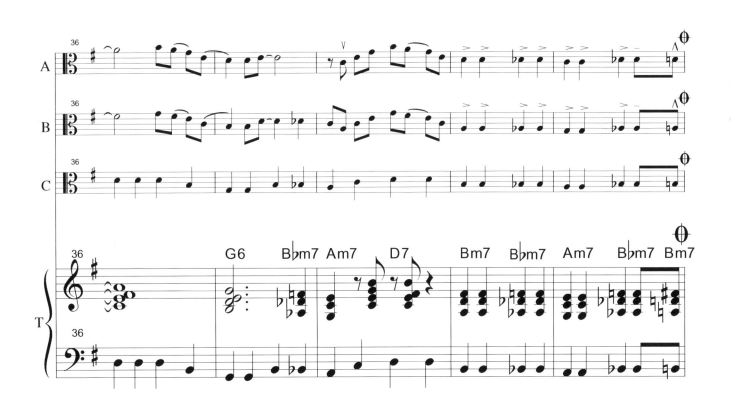

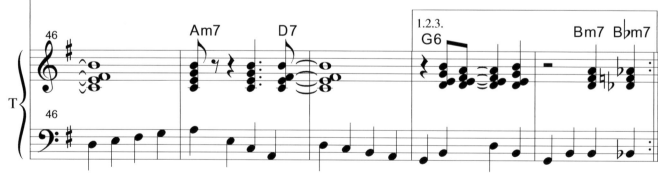

LESSON 4:
IMPROVISING WITH ONE NOTE CHANGING

Improvisers have to be aware of chord changes in the accompaniment parts. The chords in the accompaniment tell the soloist which scales to use when improvising. Sometimes the scales vary by only one or two notes.

In this lesson we use the E minor pentatonic scale but change a note on the second chord. When you see the chord symbol Em above the music you play the normal scale with B, but when you see the chord symbol C7, change the B to a B-flat. This lesson prepares you to improvise on "Canta Island," which is built on a rock feel. The eighth notes should therefore be played evenly, not swung as in previous lessons.

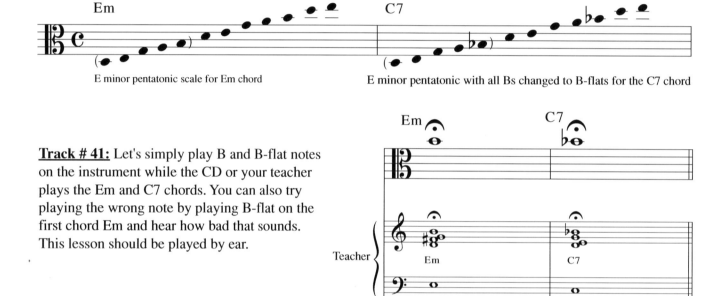

E minor pentatonic scale for Em chord

E minor pentatonic with all Bs changed to B-flats for the C7 chord

Track # 41: Let's simply play B and B-flat notes on the instrument while the CD or your teacher plays the Em and C7 chords. You can also try playing the wrong note by playing B-flat on the first chord Em and hear how bad that sounds. This lesson should be played by ear.

Track # 42: Let's groove by adding rhythms. Repeat the rhythms from the CD or your teacher, but remember the note change from B to B-flat when the chord changes from Em to C7!
(Teacher: use this or similar piano accompaniment in the following exercises.)

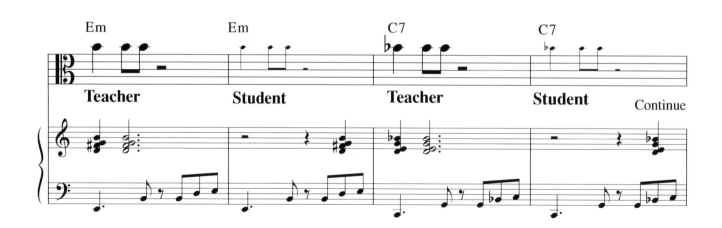

Track # 43: Let's add another couple of notes from the scale to our Bs and B-flats. Again try to imitate the CD or your teacher:

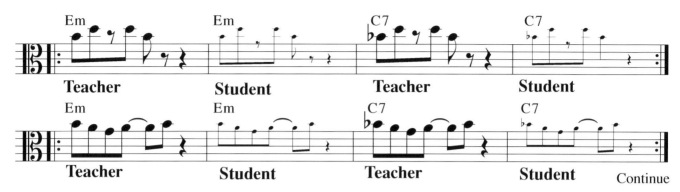

Track # 44: This time we incorporate the Bs and B-flats but start on a different note:

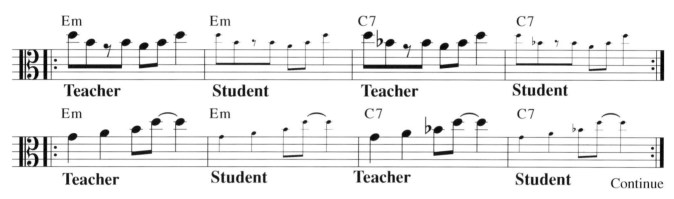

Track # 45: Play the full scales on the D and A strings with your teacher or the CD:

Track # 46: Try adding rhythms to the scale as we did in Lesson 3. This time listen for the first four measures then answer by making up your own rhythms on the scale:

Track # 47: Now try changing direction before reaching the top or bottom of the scale (remember the open D is also in the scale). Also try starting on notes other than E. The following exercise is structured like Track # 46 with the student answering the CD every four measures with an improvised phrase different from the teacher phrase:

E starting note:

Track # 48: This time play a different rhythm on C7 than on Em, and try to add skips. Watch out that you still stay within the scale:

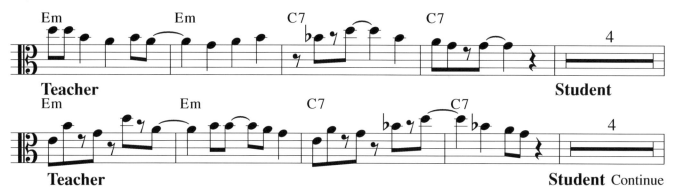

Track # 49: The following track demonstrates how to make all four measures one long sentence or phrase. That is, don't let the chord change break up your idea. This is referred to as "phrasing over the barline" and helps make the solo more interesting:

CD continues with a regular fusion rock solo

Track # 50: Go for it! This track has no solo instrument. You can practice soloing on "Canta Island." In your solo use the changing note, different rhythms, and try phrasing over the barline.

LESSON 4 (ADVANCED): USING THE FULL REGISTER

The following is for more advanced students. The solo in "Canta Island" can easily be played without the material below.

Track # 51: Try expanding the scales to all strings. Play the scale in eighth notes starting on E on the D string every two measures and changing direction at the top and bottom of your register in first position. First ascending then descending. This exercise is different in the violin edition. The CD corresponds with the violin edition only. Use Track # 50 (backup only) to play using your entire register in first position.

Ascending scale:

Descending scale:

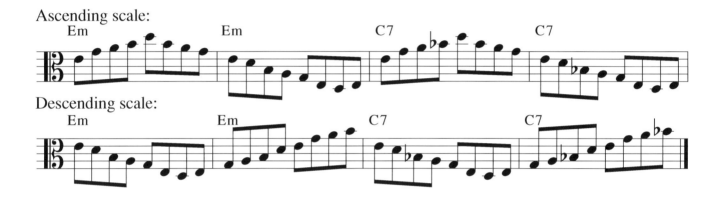

Track # 52: Stay in eighth notes and see if you can change direction within each two-measure phrase. Play along with the track but continue when the violin stops:

Track # 53: This time add rhythms and skips and use different start notes. Answer the teacher phrase with a new improvised four-measure line as we did on Track # 47:

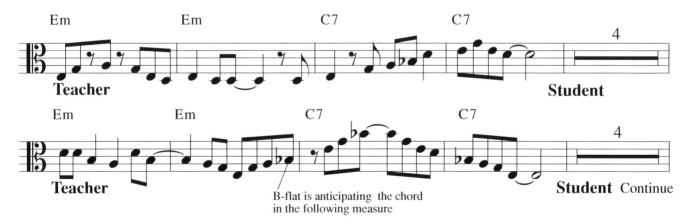

B-flat is anticipating the chord in the following measure

CANTA ISLAND

Line A

M. Norgaard

Last time D.S. al Coda without repeats

Line B

CANTA ISLAND

Funk Rock ♩ = 110

M. Norgaard

Last time D.S. al Coda without repeats

(CD repeats solo 4 times)

(play background as needed)

Solos

CANTA ISLAND

Line C

Funk Rock ♩ = 110

M. Norgaard

Last time D.S. al Coda without repeats

CANTA ISLAND

46

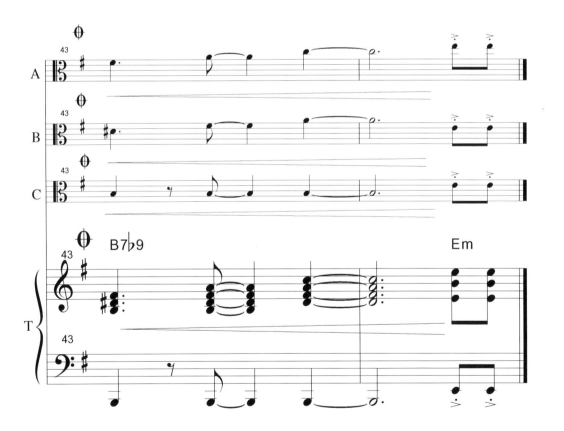

ABOUT THE AUTHOR

A performer and recording artist, Martin Norgaard is on the faculties of Belmont University's School of Music and Vanderbilt University's Blair School of Music. A member of the acoustic bluegrass/swing/rock band Acoustic Room, which records for Major Records, he leads his own jazz groups in New York and Nashville and has performed with artists as diverse as Rich McCready, Buddy Spicher, and Matt King. In addition to his *Jazz Fiddle Wizard* and *Jazz Fiddle Wizard Junior* books, Martin is the author of Mel Bay's transcriptions of Bonnie Rideout's Scottish fiddle record *Kindred Spirits*, Aubrey Haynie's *Doin' My Time*, and Mel Bay's *French Tangos for Violin* and *The Greatest Stars of Bluegrass Music* (fiddle edition). One of Martin's own solos is transcribed in the *Master Anthology of Fiddle Solos, Vol. 1*, also published by Mel Bay. After studying at the University of Copenhagen and the New England Conservatory, Martin earned his baccalaureate and master's degrees in jazz performance from William Paterson University in New Jersey and Queens College in New York, respectively.

In demand as a workshop clinician, Martin has taught or presented at the 2002 South Carolina Suzuki Institute, 2002 ASTA WITH NSOA National Studio Teachers Forum, 2002 Indiana Music Educators Association Conference, 2002 International Association for Jazz Education Conference, 2001 and 2002 Swing Week at Augusta Heritage Center and 2003 ASTA National Convention. As director of the Belmont Jazz String Quartet, he has appeared at the 2002 MENC National Conference, 2001 International Association for Jazz Education Conference, and 2001 Tennessee Music Educators Association Conference.

ABOUT THE EDITOR

Laura Reed has served as the editor of the *American String Teacher* journal of the American String Teachers Association with National School Orchestra Association and of the *American Music Teacher* journal of Music Teachers National Association. She has worked as an editor for the St. Louis and Pittsburgh Symphonies, and was a senior news representative for the University of Pittsburgh. She holds a bachelor's degree in music from the University of Cincinnati College-Conservatory of Music and is completing a master's degree in music education from West Virginia University. She currently teaches strings at Poplar Grove Middle School in Franklin, Tennessee and has taught at John F. Kennedy Middle School in Antioch, Tennessee, a suburb of Nashville.

Made in the USA
San Bernardino, CA
20 October 2017